This book is dedicated to my loving wife, Lisa, my daughters, Shannon and Lee, my son, Rich, and to my five wonderful grandsons in happy memories of all the fun we've had together.

About the Author, Richard Moody:

Richard was born in the town of Fleet in the county of Hampshire in southern England and spent his early childhood in Simon's Town outside Cape Town in South Africa. After school in South Africa, he was a student at two boarding schools in England before attending Britannia Royal Naval College, Dartmouth - the Royal Navy's equivalent of the US Naval Academy in Annapolis Maryland.

After receiving his commission as a Naval Officer in the Royal Navy and serving in the Fishery Protection Squadron, he was appointed as a Navigator and the Meteorologist on the Royal Yacht Britannia for Her Majesty the Queen's Royal Tours of Fiji, New Zealand and Australia before receiving his Wings with the Royal Navy. He flew as a pilot onboard two Royal Navy aircraft carriers operating in the Far East over a four year period with time also spent operating from shore bases in Singapore, Hong Kong, Malaysia and Western Australia.

He was then sent to fly with the US Navy during the Vietnam era and was a member of the first staff of the Navy Fighter Weapons School (TOPGUN) in San Diego California. After a final two year aircraft carrier tour with the Royal Navy in the Mediterranean and the Eastern Atlantic, he retired as a Lieutenant Commander RN after 15 years of service and became an international airline pilot with British Overseas Airways Corporation (BOAC) flying to many countries throughout the world.

Taking early retirement from BOAC, he flew with St Lucia Airways in the Caribbean before working for two years in industrial distribution in Indiana. He was subsequently hired as an International Aviation Reinsurance Broker in New York and worked in that industry for over 25 years. He also continued flying as a fighter pilot with the Royal Naval Reserve (Air) Branch for a further 12 years in Europe.

About 20 years ago, he became an ardent peace activist and joined the Coalition for Peace Action in Princeton, New Jersey, and has been a Quaker for a number of years. He is now very active in the name of Peace worldwide and works continuously to reduce US militarism and the death and destruction which is being carried out by the USA, and other countries, around the world.

He is an ardent preservationist and historian and has led historical walking tours in both Cranbury and Princeton in New Jersey for their respective Historical Societies. He also gives talks on many subjects, including New Jersey and the Revolutionary War, Alexander Hamilton, the Marquis de Lafayette and Slavery and the Underground Railroad in New Jersey etc. He has also tutored geography, history and essay writing in the adult education program at the Trenton Area Soup Kitchen (TASK) and is currently teaching geography in HomeFront's Hire Expectations program for those adults who have yet to obtain their New Jersey High School Diplomas. He is also a volunteer with the InterfaithRISE Refugee program out of the Reformed Church in Highland Park, New Jersey.

His volunteering abroad has included teaching in the Peruvian Andes and in the Black Townships in Cape Town, South Africa, and working in a Syrian Refugee Camp in Greece and he has spent time with his sponsored families and in their schools in El Salvador, Nicaragua and Bolivia. In addition to these three countries, he has also sponsored families in Mali, Senegal, Nepal, Colombia and the Philippines. He has lived in five countries - most recently in France for 10 months - and has visited over 130 countries overall. Richard has dual nationality - British and American - and considers himself to be a Global Citizen.

HERE, THERE AND EVERYWHERE

A Potpourri of Past and Present

by Richard Moody

<u>Front Cover</u>

A diverse Potpourri of multi-coloured petals.

DORRANCE PUBLISHING CO
EST. 1920
PITTSBURGH, PENNSYLVANIA 15238

Dorrance Publishing Co
585 Alpha Drive
Pittsburgh, PA 15238
Visit our website at *www.dorrancebookstore.com*

ISBN: 979-8-89027-389-5
eISBN: 979-8-89027-887-6

Chapters

Elstree School, Berkshire, England

Elstree School is an English preparatory school founded in 1848 in Elstree - a suburb to the northwest of London - which moved to Woolhampton in Berkshire in 1939 at the start of World War II.

I went to Elstree as a boarder in 1949 at the age of eight and left at age 13 to board at my public school - Marlborough College. Boarding at the age of eight was perfectly normal at that time and the majority of my friends, who went to private schools, did so.

Before I talk about the pleasures of being at Elstree, I should first explain the differences between English "prep" and "public" schools from those in America as some of my readers may be from the USA. A prep school in England is a fee paying preparatory school which prepares students for public school. However, a public school is, in fact, a private boarding high school for students aged 13 to 18. And to add to the confusion, my public school - Marlborough - was a boys only College, not unlike other public schools in England such as Eton College and Winchester College which are not colleges in the American sense. Marlborough is now co-ed and Kate, wife of William, Prince of Wales, went there.

Elstree School's move to the countryside at the start of the war was due to the school being requisitioned by the War Department and it was able to relocate to beautiful Woolhampton House - a 17th century built estate - about 50 miles to the west of London and not far from the market town of Newbury. Woolhampton House had been owned by a Polish count - Count Gurowski - whose grandson, Count R.B.M. Gurowski, known to all of us as Guro, was with me at this delightful school.

Elstree School eventually went co-ed but not until 2020 and the current number of students, which stands at around 250, has approximately 25% girls with some girls boarding from the age of nine. Children from the age of three now go to Elstree and these figures compare with a total of around 80 boys only when I was there with the youngest being eight years old.

The school - the old Woolhampton House - sat, and still sits, on about 150 acres of beautiful parkland with two large ponds. It had a walled vegetable garden and a Ha Ha, which is still there, to stop the cows and sheep from encroaching on the playing fields. The term Ha Ha goes back to the 18th century and is a sunken ditch with a stone wall on one side and I don't ever remember any of the animals intruding on to the cricket pitch so the Ha Ha must have done a good job. The two ponds, then known as Big Pond and Little Pond, were more akin to lakes and were stocked with carp and roach so fishing was very popular when we had time to spare when not in the classroom or on the playing fields.

Amazingly, I was blissfully happy the moment I moved in at Elstree at that young age and I then spent the rest of my childhood away from home at both Elstree and Marlborough. There were three terms each year at Elstree and our parents were only allowed to come to the school once a term on a Sunday to take us out but not to go home. However, we did have very long winter, spring and summer holidays (vacations in America) and none of us young lads ever thought it was strange that we didn't go home during term time.

A variety of sports were played every afternoon, and in the evening in summer, and matches were played against other prep schools on Wednesday afternoons and on Saturdays - schools such as Cheam where King Charles III went. Cricket, Football (Soccer), Rugby and Hockey (Boys Field Hockey) were the primary sports but we did swim at a local Catholic public school as we didn't have a pool at Elstree. Amazingly, we swam in the nude and none of us thought that this was the slightest peculiar!

The Headmaster was a retired Lieutenant Commander in the Royal Navy, whose family had run Elstree since 1869 and did so for 100 years, and the Commander took sports very seriously as he had been the Navy's squash champion. The story goes that the game of squash was started at the old Estree in the late 1800s when the boys would hit a soft rubber ball against the Chapel wall as a warm up for the very popular game of racquets which is still played at the Racquet and Tennis Club in New York, in Philadelphia and in Tuxedo to the north of New York City and at clubs and public schools in England.

Us youngsters had nicknames for all the Masters and for some reason the Headmaster was called Cheese and his wife was called Saggers! There were no females on the teaching staff although there was a lady who came to the school a few days a week to teach the piano and Cheese's mother taught us bible study on Sunday evenings after we had gone to the local village church for the Church of England Sunday service. Other Masters had nicknames such as Hewbie and Hobbo and I remember the school nurse was thought to be having an affair with one of the Masters. Cheese became Headmaster in 1935 and retired in 1969 after nearly 35 years of wonderful service to the school and the boys. My parents had sent me to Elstree due to my father's friendship with Cheese from their time together in the Royal Navy.

All students were taught Latin and some Greek plus the usual English, Mathematics and, most important of all, Geography and History. There were exams at the end of each term with the Common Entrance exam being taken towards the end of the final year in order to be accepted to a public school - the most popular public school being Harrow School for which Elstree has had strong connections going back many years.

On Sundays, we were required to write letters home with fountain pen, ink and blotting paper - our only means of communication with our parents as no phone calls were allowed to be made and, of course, none of us had mobile phones. All letters home were read and approved by Cheese before being posted (mailed). Cheese also read a nonfiction story to the senior boys in his study on Sunday evenings and he often gave puberty talks to those who had reached that stage in life.

One day a week, a lady came to teach us ballroom dancing and, in addition to the Waltz and Foxtrot, she taught us such as the Gay Gordons and the Dashing White Sergeant. As there were no girls at Elstree, one boy had to dance as the girl in the pairs dancing and, for some reason, I always danced as the boy and another boy, named Ben, was my partner. Ben and I subsequently played racquets against each other when I was at Marlborough and he was at Winchester. Another event that I once took part in was the school play where I played the part of the Butler to the Lord of the Manor and my only line was "Sausages Sir - all hot and bothered"!

The post WWII food, during a time of rationing, must have been pretty ghastly as many boys developed boils which we thought nothing of but the best part of eating in the dining room was a contest we played as to who could flick the most butter pats to stick on the ceiling with the very flexible knives we were given.

We had a cobbler named Stan who looked after our shoes and our football and rugby boots and who also whitened our cricket boots before matches. Stan lived in the cellar next to the boiler room and the room at the school where the boots and shoes are now kept is named Stan's Room. I played on the cricket team as a leg break bowler (my American readers can look that one up!) and also as scrum half on the rugby team, right wing on the football team and at inside left on the hockey team.

We also had a carpenter known as Carpy and it seemed his main role in life was to make butter pats which Cheese used to spank us with for minor infringements but Carpy also made the canes that Cheese used on us for more serious misdemeanours. Cheese always kept his canes in the tall cupboard (closet) in his study wrapped in tissue paper! Being a champion squash player with a very strong right hand, Cheese wielded his cane with great power and skill and it was best to avoid being naughty enough to warrant one of Cheese's canings!

Some of the better known Old Estree Boys are Robert Fellowes - now Lord Fellowes - who played on the 1st Eleven cricket team with me as an off break bowler (check that one out too) and subsequently became Her Majesty the Queen's Private Secretary. His wife is Princess Diana's elder sister. James Blunt, the very successful British pop star, also went to Elstree and, in addition to the Polish Count's grandson, other students at Elstree included the novelist Sebastian Faulks and Jack Churchill, Sir Winston's younger brother. The Honourable Patrick Connolly-Carew, who later became the 7th Baron Carew and represented Ireland in equestrian events in two Olympics, was also at Elstree with me.

I now would have never sent our son away to boarding school at the age of eight but it was considered the normal thing to do in those far off days and I was extremely happy during my five years at Elstree and thought nothing of it. It's nice to know that Elstree is still going strong and it's exciting to know that it's now accepting girls. Life at an English prep school in the 1950s was probably not too dissimilar to what went on in the 1850s but I very much doubt that Butter Pats and Canes are still in use!

European Jaunts
by Jalopy and Scooter

My long time best friend, David, and I were born three days apart in Fleet, Hampshire, in southern England where we grew up. When we were 18, we decided that summer to borrow David's sister's Lambretta scooter and head across the English Channel and explore France and southern Spain on the Mediterranean. As I had no scooter licence, I would have to ride shotgun on the pillion seat behind David which I did for the entire trip. Lambretta scooters were made by Innocenti in Milano, Italy, and named after the Lambro River and they were first cousins of the Vespa scooter.

So we drove to a small airport in Kent called Lydd and flew across the Channel to Le Touquet in France in a Bristol Freighter twin-engined piston cargo plane operated by Silver City Airways. Silver City had started life in Australia flying cargo for mining companies - in particular those in Broken Hill whose nickname is still Silver City. Hence, the airline's name. The Bristol Freighter was a very clumsy beast with a large fat nose which had two doors that opened so that cars, motorbikes and scooters could ride up a ramp into the nose and on into the body of the aircraft for the short flight across the Channel.

After the 20 minute flight, we headed to Paris on our scooter and stayed a few nights in a lovely old hotel named the Hotel des Deux Continents on Rue Jacob in St Germain-des-Pres on the Rive Gauche (Left Bank) of the river Seine. Amazingly, our room for two cost us the equivalent of 10 shillings per night which would be around 60 cents at today's dollar to pound rate of exchange. A few years ago, my wife, Lisa, and I stayed the night again in the Deux Continents and not much had changed although it was no longer 10 shillings per night!

Riding at our maximum speed of around 50 mph, we meandered down France to the Mediterranean and crossed over into Spain and spent some time in the lovely old coastal town of Cadaques on the Costa Brava - close to where the artist Salvador Dali lived in the village of Port Lligat. Then it was back into France and up to Calais where we caught the cross channel ferry across La Manche (The Sleeve as the French call the English Channel) to Dover and back home to Fleet. And, of course, we didn't wear helmets throughout the trip - nobody did in those days!

The following summer, when we were now aged 19, I bought an old jalopy - a 1937 Standard Ensign four door stick shift saloon for 25 pounds sterling which would be the equivalent of around $30 today. The Ensign was an amazing car as the bonnet (the hood) was readily detachable and the windscreen (the windshield) was hinged horizontally along the top and could be opened at any time by cranking a small handle which sat on the top of the dashboard.

This time, we took the ferry from Dover to Boulogne having met an Italian of our age, Paolo Evangelisti, on the dock at Dover who was looking for a ride across the Channel as passengers without vehicles were not allowed to ride the ferry on their own. We offered Paolo a seat in our jalopy and, after berthing in Boulogne, we drove him to Compiegne where he had left his motorbike which needed repairs. Interestingly, Compiegne is where the Germans signed their surrender in 1918 and the French in 1940 - in the same railway carriage. On saying farewell to Paolo, he insisted that we visit his family in Torino in Italy which we subsequently did.

We then headed south to Montelimar - home of delicious nougat - and on down to the Mediterranean where we water skied at Juan-les-Pins and went scuba diving with Jacques Cousteau's school in Beaulieu sur Mer. This was an exciting experience but our diving guide took us two amateurs far too deep and we both suffered from subsequent very painful earaches. It was then up the Cote d'Azur to Monaco and Monte Carlo before crossing into Italy and on to Torino to see Paolo's parents. They gave us a warm welcome and I remember that his father got out his slide rule (these were the days before electronic calculators) and calculated which bank we should go to in order to obtain the best exchange rate for us to convert our pounds into lira. Meanwhile, Paolo's mother had cooked us the world's most delicious red, yellow and orange peppers which we'd never had before in post-war England.

It then required our struggling jalopy to carry us over the Alps into Switzerland. Initially, all went well but, as the roads became steeper and steeper, our old jalopy was getting slower and slower. Eventually, when we were passed by a horse and cart on a mountain pass, we realized something needed to be done. David, being a bit of a mechanic, decided to take the bonnet off and crank open the windshield. All the while, I was struggling to get us going a bit faster to no avail. David, who was now leaning out of the front window and attempting to do running repairs, soon discovered that the accelerator cable was loose. Tightening it up, we were back in action again and we soon waved goodbye to the horse and cart as we slowly accelerated over the Alps. We had purchased a large demijohn water jug in Spain and David, still leaning out of the front window, poured water on the struggling hot engine which helped us along the way but perhaps that was not the most sensible action to have taken!

After Switzerland, we struggled on to Heilbron, between Heidelberg and Stuttgart in Germany, where David's sister lived with her German husband. We were desperately short of cash and David's sister came to the rescue and funded our return to England via the ferry from Dunkirk to Dover. Sadly, my 1937 Ensign didn't last much longer as it broke down when

I was driving back to start the school year at Britannia Royal Naval College in Dartmouth in Devonshire. Leaving it beside the road and hitchhiking the rest of the way to the Naval College, I subsequently learned that my dear old friend had been towed away and ceremoniously left on a rubbish dump (trash heap)!

Life was very different in those far off days and some of the fun and games we carried out as teenagers would now be considered to be beyond foolish but we enjoyed every minute of it and we lived to fight another day.

A Hitchhiker's Guide to the Grecians
(with all due respect to Douglas Adams)

Many moons ago, at the end of my tour of duty on Queen Elizabeth's Royal Yacht Britannia, where I had been Her Majesty's Meteorologist and Celestial Ocean Navigator for the Royal Tours of Fiji, New Zealand and Australia, I and two of my fellow, very junior, Royal Navy Yachtsmen (Yotties) officers decided to rent a place to stay in Greece for three weeks of relaxation after the rigorous routines of Royal protocol. My time onboard Britannia is the subject of Chapter Four of my book - "Flying through Life - From Fighter Pilot to Peace Activist".

One of my two Naval companions was an Australian on loan from the Royal Australian Navy who sadly passed away some years ago. The other Yottie friend ended up as Inspector General with the United Nations High Commissioner for Refugees (UNHCR) - in particular during the conflict in the Balkans in the 1990s and he and his team were subsequently awarded the Nobel Peace Prize.

We ended up in the small seaside community of Kalamaki Beach which is approximately eight miles south of Athens and not far from the village of Vouliagmeni. We rented an attractive villa apartment for the six of us - the others being my Australian friend's girlfriend, her cousin and his sister who were with us in our two cars - one a classic white Jaguar and the other a British Racing Green Triumph Spitfire. But not in my ancient jalopy that had seen better days. We drove down through Europe and Yugoslavia, as the Balkans were then named, over a three day period and arrived none the worse for wear having slept one night on a beach on the Adriatic Sea close to the northern Greek border.

However, I was only able to stay in Greece for two weeks as I had to get back to dear old Blighty to start Royal Navy Flying Training with the Royal Air Force in Yorkshire so I decided that, without a car of my own, it would be a jolly wheeze if I hitchhiked the approximate 2,000 miles in order to start my flying appointment on the designated start date. This venture ended up taking six days involving a copious number of thumbed car rides, two ferries, two trains and one truck and one motorbike.

On the first day of my adventure, one of my villa mates kindly drove me to the town of Corinth, where I began my hitchhiking with a ride to Patras, which is on the southern shore of the Gulf of Corinth about 130 miles to the west of Athens. There, I caught the ferry which took me up the west coast of Greece to the port town of Igoumenitsa and then across the narrow stretch of water to the island of Kerkyra (Corfu). From there, my ferry headed across the Adriatic Sea to Brindisi on the heel of Italy. That's where my hitchhiking started in earnest - heading up through Italy, past San Marino, into Switzerland and France and across the English Channel to England.

Within an hour of stepping off my ferry in Brindisi, I had managed to flag down four rides - one of whom being a motorcyclist. Not surprisingly, neither he nor I wore a helmet which would be considered very foolish today but he took me to Bari which is about 100 miles north of Brindisi where the highlight of my six day adventure began.

As I stood by the side of the road wondering if my luck would continue, a large behemoth of a truck/lorry pulled up and the two drivers in the cab waved me aboard. The cab had a large area behind the two front seats with a bunk bed and this became my home for most of the next three days as we trundled up the east coast of Italy and past San Marino (a tiny Republic landlocked by Italy) and Rimini. My Italian drivers were named Luigi and Musso and, every time we stopped for a bite to eat at a truck stop, they insisted that they pay for my meal. On we went up the Italian coast before turning northwest to Bologna and on to Milano where I sadly had to say farewell to my two new "amici" who had delighted me with fascinating stories in their broken English. Whenever one of the drivers needed to rest up, I vacated my bunk for him and, instead, sat in his place on the right front seat of the cab with the driver on my left.

Luckily, I soon picked up another ride in Milano and that driver, and then another, took me into Switzerland and dropped me off late at night at the Lucerne train station. With no trains into France until the next morning, I slept the night on an uncomfortable wooden bench on the platform and caught an early morning train to Basel in France on the Swiss border where my hitchhiking exploits began again. After a number of local car rides, I was picked up by a US Air Force sergeant who was heading to Metz in Alsace Lorraine in France. After arriving in this mid-sized city, I decided I deserved a night in a nice hotel so I treated myself to a delicious French dinner, washed down with some cheap vin rouge, and spent a blissful night in a cozy double bed.

The next morning, it was time to head towards the English Channel (La Manche - The Sleeve - en Francais) and a few more rides found me in Calais in order to catch the ferry to Dover in Kent - the English county where my aunt lived in the village of Beckley. But, alas, I was not allowed to buy a ticket on the ferry since I was a solo passenger without a car. There was no Eurotunnel train service in those days for me to take and I was therefore flummoxed as to my next move when, lo and behold, a car drove up with none other than an old friend of mine from Marlborough College at the wheel. He had been commissioned in the British Army and was on his way home to England after a vacation in France with two of his fellow officers. "Jump in" he cried and I had a pleasant short trip, sitting in his car on the ferry, across the Channel to Dover. There, my mobile saviour then drove me to the village in Kent where I stayed with my aunt before heading back to my home in Hampshire by train and on up to Yorkshire for my flying training.

Sadly, hitchhiking in today's world is a thing of the past although, until COVID, it was totally accepted in our old town of Crested Butte, Colorado, where it was considered very impolite not to pick up hikers in search of a ride. My experience all those years ago, where I travelled through five countries under someone else's steam, is indelibly ingrained in my memory. There's nothing like being a travelling hobo through so much diverse culture and finding luck to be on one's side and friendliness to be in so many people's souls. And how is it that I can still remember Luigi's and Musso's names after all those passing years?

Pubs and Pub Life in England

The Pub, or Public House, often known as The Local, is the favorite watering hole and centre of social life in a majority of English towns and villages with the landlord being known as the Publican - which is not a political title!

The Romans were the first to have establishments selling alcohol in the form of wine and vine leaves were often hung above the doorway as a sign as to what was available inside. But it was not until the Middle Ages that pubs became popular in England with beer, mead and cider being sold in great quantities to the villagers and to those stopping by in their coaches and on their horses. Today, some of the pubs are Free Houses which, sadly, does not mean that the libations are free to consume. It merely means that that pub is not tied to any particular brewery but is free to sell whatever make of beer it chooses.

There are a vast number of pub names and signs going back hundreds of years with one of the oldest names being the "White Hart". An Act was passed in 1393 stating that all drinking establishments must identify themselves as such and a White Hart was the personal badge of King Richard II who was on the throne of England at that time. The "Rose and Crown" is another popular pub sign - so named when Henry VII ended the War of the

Roses in 1485 and united the Houses of Lancaster and York by marrying Elizabeth of York. A red rose was the symbol of the House of Lancaster and the white rose that of the House of York. Another pub name with a regal connection is the "Royal Oak" - so called after the tree where the future Charles II hid in the branches during the English Civil War. He was then the claimant to the throne of England and was subsequently crowned King Charles II after Oliver Cromwell's death.

Other pub names of interest are the "Crown" where publicans showed their loyalty to the monarch regardless of who was on the throne and many signs indicated their proximity to local agriculture and farming such as the "Barley Mow", the "Bull's Head" and the "Oatsheaf". My father died from a heart attack while drinking a gin and tonic at the Oatsheaf in the town of Fleet in Hampshire and so I always have a G & T in his honour at the Oatsheaf when back in Fleet - the town where I was born. Other practical pub sign names are the "Coach and Horses", where stage coaches would stop for the night and change horses, the "Bird in Hand" - named because of Henry VIII's love of falconry - and the "Fox and Hounds" due to the passion for hunting in the middle ages.

Other interesting pub names are the "Goat and Compasses" which is derived from the religious saying "God encompasseth us" and the "Lamb and Lark" which comes from the sixteenth century proverb - "Go to bed with the Lamb and rise with the Lark". My wife, Lisa, and I once lived in a small village in Somerset in England called Limington and our Local was indeed the "Lamb and Lark" whose publican was a retired steeplechase jockey with the appropriate name of Johnny Gamble! My public (private) high school was Marlborough College in the old market town of Marlborough in Wiltshire and our favorite pub, where we were able to drink once we achieved the age of 18, was the "Castle and Ball" - known to us dirty minded schoolboys as the "Turret and Te***cle"!

Pubs are always friendly spots for many beer-drinking old codgers, sporting lads, families and even dogs - with children being required to sit outside in the garden in the summer and in a separate room in winter. However badly dogs normally behave, they always bring their best table manners into the pub - dutifully sitting under the table waiting for morsels to come their way or for generous customers to slip a piece of meat to them when the dog's owner is playing darts.

Various games such as Quiz Nights, Chess and Backgammon are very popular and the Dart board is always in use. Many pubs have Darts teams that challenge other villages which, apart from being a lot of fun, is very good for business since darts players always improve their skills by imbibing copious amounts of beer and the contests bring many outsiders to the pub. Some pubs still have old fashioned bowling alleys, which are more akin to ancient skittles, and wagers in beer are often placed on which team will win.

A number of pubs have become rather posh and are known as Gastro Pubs and serve upmarket meals but many pubs still serve the same type of food which dates back centuries. Food such as Bacon, Sausage or Chip Butties, Scotch Eggs, Sticky Toffee Pudding, Banoffee Pie, Loaded Baked Potatoes - topped with Cheese or Tuna - and something called Eton Mess. And Roast Sunday Lunch is very popular where a large hunk of beef, lamb or pork is carved at the table and served with roast potatoes, parsnips, cabbage, carrots, peas and gravy. Enough to send you to sleep on a typically rainy English Sunday afternoon.

Lisa and I have spent many hours in country pubs - often in the North of England where the local accents are sometimes hard to decipher. One pub in Derbyshire has dear old Ron who shows up promptly at 9 pm, has two pints of local beer and then totters home to bed. Another of our favorite pubs has an old boy aged in his 90s who spends a lot of time quaffing his ale and telling stories about living in the same village and working in a local wool mill since the age of 16 - always dressed in a coat and tie.

But our best experience, which combined pub life with the local accents in the Lake District in the north of England, involved a trip with local northern friends to a pub in the middle of nowhere to savour the delicious Lamb Henry which is popular there. On approaching the pub, named the

Craven Heifer, a Land Rover was wandering all over the road and, when it stopped outside the pub, the driver approached me and said, what sounded to me, like "Go into poob and ask for a tow". So in I went but the old gaffers, sitting inside sipping their beers, could not understand my southern English accent and I had to ask my northern friend to ascertain from the driver what he'd actually said. What in fact he had said was "Go into poob and ask for me Dad whose name is Alex Towler"!

A popular beer in Yorkshire is Theakston's - one of the many types of beer which are pulled by hand from the cellar with absolutely no carbonation. Once pulled, the white head is allowed to settle and the creamy taste is beyond delicious. The story goes that the eldest son of the owner of Theakston's fell out with his father and became the black sheep of the family. Needless to say, the prodigal son formed his own brewery and named his beer Black Sheep!

As my readers can see, pub life in England is nothing but good fun, delicious ales (and wines), great games and surprisingly excellent food. Pubs are indeed very much the social gathering places in many rural communities, villages and towns and long may they be so.

Love at First Sight

When I flew to San Diego, California, from London one October to take up my duties as a fighter pilot with the US Navy (USN) out of Naval Air Station (NAS) Miramar, I was offered a room in a lovely ranch-style house close to Mission Bay with three other USN officers - one recently retired. The house had a beautiful patio with palm trees which led down to a lovely swimming pool.

One of my F4 Phantom fighter squadron roommates happened to be engaged to a lady in Fort Lauderdale, Florida, and, in those crazy Vietnam era days, pilots were able to "borrow" a squadron aircraft on Fridays and fly to anywhere in the USA for the weekend with the exception of flying to Alaska and Hawaii. Naturally, my roommate always wanted to fly to Florida to see his fiancee and, on a couple of occasions, he persuaded me to come with him in the two seat F4 in anticipation that he would fix me up with a blind date.

We would initially fly to Tinker Air Force Base (AFB) in Oklahoma City and spend Friday night there in the Bachelor Officers Quarters (BOQ) where the Officer's Club was always open to the ladies of Oklahoma City. Early the next morning, we would fly on to Homestead AFB which was not far from Fort Lauderdale. Unfortunately, my blind dates were not quite what I was looking for but my pilot friend assured me that he had just the lady for me if I came to his wedding the following June. He was referring to Lisa who was teaching at a US Army Base in Bayreuth in Germany and who would be flying across the Atlantic for his wedding. Lisa and his fiance were, and still are, staunch friends having been together at Butler University in Indianapolis, Indiana.

I subsequently flew my Phantom to the wedding on Key Biscayne south of Miami but this time I flew to NAS Key West as the runways at Homestead AFB were under repair. Renting a car in Key West, I drove up the Keys to this amazing wedding which was held in the mansion once owned by John Deere of tractor fame. Arriving at the wedding venue, I changed into my white Royal Navy officer's uniform, carried my antique Royal Navy sword and prepared for duty in the bridal Guard of Honour.

At the post-wedding reception, I spotted this gorgeous girl across the hall, grabbed two glasses of bubbly and introduced myself to Lisa who was to become my future wife. It really was "Love at first sight" and I persuaded her to postpone her trip to England, where she was heading before returning to Germany, and, instead, spend a few nights with me in my attractive house outside San Diego. This she did after I had flown my F4 back to California via NAS Oceana in Virginia and Buckley Air National Guard base in Colorado and she had jetted in from Indiana where she had been to see her parents.

We had been in each other's presence for no longer than seventy two hours when I proposed to her - an event which was heralded by one of my other roommates who, suspecting something was afoot, serenaded us outside our bedroom with love songs on his guitar. This must have worked as Lisa accepted my proposal! We then held a surprise party at our bachelor pad, which was nicknamed the P***derosa, to announce our engagement! It was the time of the Apollo 11 moon landing and four uninvited aviators gate crashed our party and gave us all surprise "moonshots" with AP-OL-LO-II painted on their nether regions!

The plan was for Lisa and I to get married in a year's time, the following June, in Indianapolis where Lisa's parents lived but we decided it might be sensible if I took some leave from the US Navy at Christmas and fly to Germany to see if we were making the right decision. After flying to Germany, Lisa picked me up at the Nuremberg airport and drove us to Bayreuth but on the way we decided not to wait until next summer to get married but to get married now. There were three choices as to location. Fly back to the USA, get married in Germany or drive to England and get married there. The USA did not seem like a good choice, as I'd just flown in from there, and we didn't have any family in Germany so we decided that dear old Blighty was the country of choice.

My grandfather had been a country Vicar in a lovely old Norman parish in Frensham in Surrey with his church dating back to the 12th century. Knowing that my English brother-in-law was the least likely to have a heart attack at this sudden turn of events, we told him the news and he had special bans read in the church which were required as our wedding was to be at very short notice. Lisa's brother and sister flew in from the USA and my mother and my immediate family came to our wedding ceremony making a total of nine family and friends in the church. We then had a much larger reception at my mother's house in Fleet in Hampshire - the house where I was born.

We had driven to England from Bayreuth in Lisa's ancient VW Beetle with a stop for the night along the way in delightful Bruges in Belgium where all the canals were frozen as it was the height of winter. Our brief honeymoon was spent in Beaulieu on the south coast of Hampshire with New Year's dinner at a lovely old inn, the Master Builder's House, in Buckler's Hard where warships had been built in Nelson's days.

Then it was the long drive back to Bayreuth and time for Lisa to resign from her teaching position and for me to fly back to San Diego and find accommodation for our first ten months together in California. Renting an apartment on the Pacific Ocean in Solana Beach to the north of San Diego, we had an idyllic introduction to married life but it was then time for me to take up my duties again with the Royal Navy so back we flew to the land of my birth for many years of unadulterated bliss. Amazingly, after close to fifty four years together, Lisa and I are still talking to each other!

My Ejection from a Burning Fighter into the Pacific Ocean

On November 10 1969, I ejected from a burning F4J Phantom fighter jet into the Pacific Ocean about three miles off the southern California coast - not far from La Jolla. I was operating out of Naval Air Station (NAS) Miramar and was leading a TOPGUN (correct spelling!) training flight when serving with the United States Navy during my time on loan from the Royal Navy. TOPGUN was the Naval Fighter Weapons School (NFWS) and I had in fact set fire to myself - but not by smoking a cigar or cigarette in the cockpit! There is a brief description of this ejection in Chapter 7 of my book entitled "Flying through Life - From Fighter Pilot to Peace Activist".

At the time of my ejection, I was the flight leader on a 2 on 1 fighter combat training sortie where my wingman was flying another F4J and the opposition - known as the "bogey" - was an A4E Skyhawk whose type was nicknamed the Mongoose. The A4E was used to simulate the MIG 17 during the Vietnam conflict as its performance was similar to that of the MIG. It is always essential in Air Combat Maneuvering (ACM) training to "fight" against opposing aircraft whose performance is dissimilar to that of one's own aircraft but similar to the opposition.

My callsign was "Cholmondeley "- pronounced Chumley - a name that dates back to William I of England's Domesday Book of 1086. Being a British Limey, I had decided that a distinctly English callsign would be more suitable for me than the more macho names, such as Viper, Gator, Condor, Cougar, Smash, Rattler and Yank etc, which my fellow US Navy TOPGUN pilots had adopted.

The F4J was a powerful fighter aircraft with two high thrust General Electric engines equipped with afterburners whereby the act of afterburning injects more fuel into the aircraft's very hot exhaust and further instantaneous ignition occurs. This results in dramatically increased thrust. In British military flying circles, the word afterburner is replaced by the perhaps more descriptive term of reheat.

The rear end of the F4 - called the empennage, a French term - carried a vast supply of aviation fuel which was used to feed the engines and also provide the fuel which was injected into the afterburning system. The empennage, comprising the vertical fin, the downward facing horizontal stabilators (known as an anhedral) and the rear end of the fuselage, was therefore a flying fuel tank as well as being part of the aircraft's aerodynamics. It's worth noting that much of the current nomenclature in aviation dates back to the early days of aviation where the French were very much in the forefront. French words such as "empennage", "aileron", "fuselage", "sortie" and "pitot" (as in pitot tube - an aerial speedometer) are still in use today.

On that eventful day about half way through a series of engagements with our two F4s "fighting" the MIG-simulating A4E, the pilot of Mongoose - callsign "Rattler" - announced over the radio that fuel was pouring from the back of my aircraft. About that time, I also had electronic warnings in my cockpit that I was losing my flying control hydraulics and my bird became extremely unstable. Shortly thereafter, "Rattler" shouted that the escaping stream of fuel was now on fire and that the fire was rapidly closing in on the rear of my aircraft. In a few seconds, the entire empennage was on fire and it was time to punch out. It was later discovered that flames from my afterburner had set fire to the stream of fuel which was escaping from a leak in the back of my aircraft and that this was the first of five similar occurrences.

I was able to turn the burning beast away from the coast and slow it down to around 250 knots (approx 290 mph) before I ordered the Radar Intercept Officer (RIO) in my back seat behind me to eject. The act of activating his ejection seat fired off our joint cockpit canopy above us before he punched out and, a few seconds later, I too ejected in my Mk 7 Martin-Baker rocket seat from the flaming inferno at a height of around 10,000 feet.

An ejection seat could be fired by pulling either of two handles - one above the head of the pilot at the top of the seat with the other being between the pilot's legs. The top handle was the handle of choice since the act of reaching up above the head and pulling down the handle over the pilot's face placed the seat occupant's back in a vertical position - the better to survive the ejection kick of 22G (twenty two times the force of gravity). The top handle also pulled a mask over the pilot's face to protect it from the air blast when the seat was blasted skywards.

The easier-to-reach, and quicker to fire, lower handle was only used in instances such as a failed catapult shot off an aircraft carrier, at very low level or when G forces prevented the pilot from being able to reach up to the top handle. Leaning forward to fire the lower handle prevented the back from being in a vertical position which often resulted in serious back issues.

The top handle is now no longer in place in most modern ejection seats with the seat being fired by using the lower handle. To prevent subsequent back injuries, a harness pulls the pilot back into the seat so the body is in a vertical position when the seat fires.

My ejection, using the top handle, was clean and successful although receiving a kick of twenty two times the force of gravity up your you-know-what is not to be recommended. The small drogue chutes, connected to the top of my seat, pulled my seat away from me after the barostatic-triggered releasing device operated and this allowed me to be automatically separated from my seat and my parachute to instantly deploy. If my ejection had occurred at a far greater height, I would have plummeted seawards in my seat until the barostatic device operated at a lower altitude and my seat would have fallen away and my parachute would have opened - as it did in my case at a lower altitude. Slowly drifting down from a height such as 30,000 feet is not a good experience for breathing and body temperature!

I was now hanging below my parachute with a grandstand view and I saw my burning fighter, with its engines roaring, rear up ahead of me in a ball of fire, do a perfect whifferdill U turn and then plunge into the Pacific 10,000 feet below me where it blew up into hundreds of flaming pieces. The act of ejecting had automatically triggered an emergency signal on my seat but I also made a call on the emergency frequency on my small radio which was part of my survival gear. My survival pack, which I was sitting on in the aircraft, came with me on my ejection and underneath it was an inflatable liferaft which would inflate when released from the survival pack on a long cord.

As I neared the surface of the ocean, I released the liferaft which immediately inflated when the tightening of the cord, due the liferaft's weight, fired a CO2 cylinder inside it. As the raft hit the water, I released my chute and plunged into the ocean with my chute thankfully blowing away. My RIO was slow to release his chute which unfortunately came down on top of him in the water leading him to have to dig out his survival knife and hack his way out from under the canopy. My clean landing allowed me to haul myself into my inflated life raft and await an anticipated pick up.

Fortunately for me, I had good luck as a Coast Guard S61 helicopter with a "boat" hull was close by and, landing in the water, it taxied up to me in my liferaft. I clambered into the helo and was flown back to NAS Miramar none the worse for wear. Amazingly, word had got out about my adventure and a local TV station was waiting to interview me once I had changed out of my wet flight suit and donned a more comfortable dry uniform. Interestingly, a piece of my aircraft, with its identification number on it, washed up on a nearby beach 30 years later.

I didn't have time to be scared during this dramatic event in my life and I was no doubt mentally prepared for such a disaster after flying supersonic jet fighters and having regular ejection seat training and also operating on and off aircraft carriers which I had done for the four years before my ejection. Not long after my ejection, I was notified by Martin-Baker that I had now become a member of the Martin-Baker Tie Club and I was sent a Martin-Baker tie. A navy blue tie embossed with the red triangular warning symbols which are on the sides of aircraft which have dangerous ejection seats.

Sadly, the long term effects of my ejection - a combination of spinal stenosis, displaced vertebrae, arthritis and age - have come home to roost and I now have a very painful back. A back issue where no specialist has been able to alleviate the pain.and a back on which none of the specialists wish to operate for fear of making my condition worse. As it was all the fault of a leaking "empennage", a flaming "fuselage" and burning "ailerons" on a "sortie", I guess I could blame our French friends for my "stenose spinale" but I'll let them off the hook. It's now just a case of "C'est la Vie"!

The Sport of Kings

Horse Racing, traditionally known as the Sport of Kings, is thought to have first been organized in the early 17th Century under King James 1 of England when two horse match races were run across country over distances of up to four miles. Not only did the King encourage the sport but he insisted that he rode his own horses even though he was a notoriously bad jockey. The majority of these races were challenges on the flat but steeplechasing also became very popular when two wealthy owners would race their horses against each other across fields, fences and ditches with the "winning post" being the church in the far distance whose steeple was a prominent landmark which could be seen from a long way away.

Over the years, racing expanded with not only groups of thoroughbreds racing against each other but also with contests in the USA involving quarter horses and standardbreds. Thoroughbreds being pure bred horses with first class pedigrees, quarter horses being bred for speed over very short distances and standardbreds being either trotters or pacers which tow a 'sulky' cart driven by a horseman known as a driver.

The earliest classic horse race was the Epsom Derby (pronounced Darby) which was first run in Surrey in England in 1780. It's reputed that the race gained its name after two noblemen, Lord Derby and Sir Charles

Bunbury, challenged each other to a race between their two finest three year old male colts on Epsom Downs in Surrey with Lord Derby's thoroughbred coming out the winner. I guess if Sir Charles' nag had won the challenge we would now have the Epsom Bunbury and no doubt the Kentucky Bunbury as well, since the Kentucky Derby, first raced in 1875, takes its name from its Epsom cousin.

Horse racing is popular in many countries around the world with the vast majority of races being run on turf unlike most of the races in the USA which are run on dirt. The USA, being a country with long distances between coasts and borders, means that horses are shipped many miles to race in many States and on arrival at a particular race track are stabled at the track for weeks on end. They are then raced in a number of races at the same track with racing taking place on most days of the week. A turf course would not survive the incessant pounding by the horses' hooves on consecutive days while dirt tracks are able to be raced on a multiple number of times over a period of time.

Unfortunately, racing in the USA promotes speed and not distance and immature two year olds are often raced too early in their careers over short distances with a number of breakdowns occurring. The often firmness of the dirt doesn't help with the well being of the horses and many fatalities also occur. And muddy dirt tracks often mean that the lead horse wins since those behind him or her in the field do not enjoy the mud being flung up in their faces. On top of this, there's no national racing governing body in the USA and the disqualification of horses after the use of drugs by individual States is weak since the larger the field the greater the revenue that a particular State is able to generate. One of the top trainers, Bob Baffert, has had over 30 horses fail drug tests over the years and his horse was disqualified from winning the Kentucky Derby due to a failed drug test not long ago.

The arrival of electronic betting with the use of iPhones, the legalization of off-course computerized betting and the introduction of casinos at US race tracks has added to the problem with many low level races now having far larger purses than they did previously. Many of the races in the USA today, known as Claiming races, are of a low standard where a horse can be sold before the race at a cheap price but the purse money for the race is higher than it ever was in the past due to the current casino revenue. Hence, horses of poor quality are now entered in these races and rogue trainers sometimes drug injured or unfit horses in an attempt to win the now much higher winning purses.

Sadly, live horse racing has lost its appeal to many of the public in the USA and the number of spectators at racetracks nationwide has dropped considerably since the heyday of racing in the '70s and '80s when thousands would flock to the tracks to see the horses themselves in the parade ring before the race and then watch the horse race from the stands instead of on TV in the casino. On top of this, few punters appear to have any interest in the name of the horse itself, and its breeding, with many punters only able to identify their horse by its number and not its name. However, huge crowds of up to 150,000 still flock to Churchill Downs in Kentucky for the classic Kentucky Derby which is often called the most exciting two minutes in racing. Unfortunately, racing in the USA suffered more bad publicity in May 2023 when eight horses died either training or racing at Churchill Downs burning the run up to the Kentucky Derby.

Since James 1's introduction, racing in the British Isles and Ireland has flourished over the centuries although it appears that the onset of electronic betting is now too starting to take its toll on racecourse attendances. However, the big meetings in England at such as Royal Ascot, Epsom, York and Goodwood on the flat, and the steeplechasing Festival at Cheltenham, still see large crowds when the social side of horse racing also comes to the fore with copious amounts of Champagne and Pimms being imbibed in addition to the placing of large bets on the totalisator (paris mutuel pool betting) and with the fixed odds bookmakers. Interestingly, one race meeting in Ireland at Laytown runs its races on a beach and there is also racing at St Moritz in Switzerland on snow.

France is at the forefront of European thoroughbred racing with its famous tracks of ParisLongchamp, Chantilly, St Cloud and Deauville plus the many other rural courses dotted around the country. Whereas the racecourses in the British Isles have bookmakers and the tote, French betting revenue relies only on the tote-style Pari Mutuel Urbain (PMU) which makes betting available in all bars and newsagents/tabacs as well as at the hippodrome (racecourse). The resulting commissions ensure very high purses, free parking at the courses, free entry and a free program with a form guide. Plus a delicious meal in the restaurant overlooking the winning post at a low cost is not to be missed.

Races in the USA are run over shorter distances than in many other countries with the third Classic, the Belmont Stakes, being run over the longest Classic distance - a mile and a half - with few other races in the USA being run over that distance - or even further. The Belmont Stakes was first run at Jerome Park in the Bronx in 1867 while the longest stakes race at Saratoga (founded in 1863) is also over one and a half miles. By comparison, the fifth of the English Classics, the St Leger (1776), is run over one and three quarter miles and the renowned Ascot Gold Cup (1807) is a long distance race of two and a half miles. The steeplechase that galvanizes the British is the Grand National run over slightly longer than four and a quarter miles while the flat race in Australia, which is known as "The Race that stops the Nation", is the Melbourne Cup (1861) run over two miles.

Unknown to many is the steeplechase racing in the USA which takes place mostly in Maryland, Virginia, New Jersey and the Carolinas with the Maryland Hunt Cup being the most famous race. One lovely little jumping track is Fair Hill in Maryland which was inaugurated in 1926 by William du Pont Jr. With tote betting, a large stand for spectators, a barn-like restaurant serving delicious crab cakes and great horse racing, Fair Hill is a must for all those who are interested in horses and steeplechasing. However, it currently holds only one day's racing a year - on the Saturday of Memorial Day weekend - but plans are afoot to add more days racing at this lovely venue.

My ardent love of horse racing dates back to my school days in England where, amazingly, I was able to open an account with a local bookmaker in the town of Marlborough in Wiltshire when I was in boarding high school. Many years later, I had my own owner's colours registered with the English Jockey Club and the French France Galop and they were a combination of the Stars and Stripes and the Union Jack - being Red and White Stripes, Blue Sleeves and Blue Cap with White Stars. My experience as an owner is best left for another time!

Interestingly, an English trainer friend was also equine advisor to an Arab sheik who owned horses trained by one of the top trainers in France, Jean-Claude Rouget. JCR trains in Normandy and also near the Pau racecourse, not far from Biarritz and close to where my wife, Lisa, and I lived for ten months in southwest France. After being introduced to him by my English trainer friend, I think JCR was convinced that I wanted to buy a thoroughbred and have it trained by him. Why else would he have invited me to watch early morning workouts of his string of horses, entertain us at the Pau races and come to our village of Salies de Bearn to dine with us? I must have been a big disappointment to JCR but not long ago he celebrated his 7,000th winner on racecourses in Europe and the British Isles.

When the usual betting layabouts in our local bar in Salies, the Cafe des Thermes, learned of my JCR connection, I was always greeted at the door with a beer - usually by Charlie, a local chef - in the hope that I would then reveal the likelihood of a JCR winner. This often allowed my gambling friends to place a winning bet on the PMU while watching the race on TV in the cafe which was always tuned to les Hippodromes when racing was in progress. Following JCR proved to be financially successful for me and I left France well in pocket after my many bets on JCR's winners.

In addition to the lovely racing in France, I've also enjoyed racing in England. Wales, Scotland, the USA, Canada, Argentina, Australia, Singapore, Hong Kong, Mexico and South Africa. The latter when I lived there as a boy and also when I went back there with the Royal Navy and when Lisa and I were teaching in the Black Townships outside Cape Town not long ago. One of the top trainers was the son of one of my English racing friends.

A final sidebar of note involves Pau and the Wright brothers. After their initial flight at Kitty Hawk in North Carolina in 1903, Wilbur and Orville repaired to France which was very much in the forefront during the early days of aviation. After demonstrating flying near Le Mans, the two brothers set up a flight school in 1909 on what is now the racecourse at Pau on a strip of land known as Long Pont. In recognition of these two pioneers, a full size replica of their Wright Flyer aeroplane sits on a roundabout (rond-point) not far from the Pau racecourse. As you can see, my aviation career and my love of horse racing are not too far apart. I only wish that US horse racing and its supporters and organisers would see the need to bring the actual horse and its breeding - and not an electronic substitute - back into the forefront of this ancient sport.

The Khyber Pass
and the Valley of Swat

After my time as a fighter pilot with the Royal Navy and the United States Navy, I decided to try my luck as an international airline pilot with British Overseas Airways Corporation (BOAC) since this would mean flying to many locations around the world.

So I signed on and flew a lovely airliner - the Super VC 10 - in which we covered the majority of the world except for South America and West Africa. I say that the VC 10 was lovely since it was a joy to fly, easy to land in cross winds and very manoeuverable. It was manufactured by a British company - Vickers Armstrong - and could carry over 200 passengers. Powered by four Rolls Royce Conway engines, it had a maximum ceiling of 43,000 feet, was capable of speeds of close to 600 mph and had a range of approximately 5,000 miles. Its range meant that it could fly non-stop from London to cities such as Nairobi in Kenya, Chicago and Mexico City and it once held the fastest airline subsonic transatlantic crossing time of five hours which was only surpassed when the supersonic Concorde came into operation. The VC 10 had a smooth, glamorous look about it with its four engines sitting in pairs at the rear end of the fuselage below its attractive high T-shaped tail with its vertical fin and swept back horizontal stabilators. After its service as a civilian airliner with a number of African and Middle Eastern airlines, in addition to BOAC, it was converted to an aerial tanker and used as such by the Royal Air Force (RAF) and other nations' military wings.

One of my most memorable trips with BOAC was an eight day bonanza from May 3 to 11 1979 flying passengers in a Super VC 10 from London to Damascus in Syria and then on for the night in Amman in Jordan before landing at our final destination - Rawalpindi in Pakistan - on May 5. In those days, airline flying was a trifle different from what it is today and, amazingly, on this trip, the flight and cabin crews had a five day layover in Rawalpindi. A trifle different than today since all passengers dressed attractively, were very polite and were allowed to visit the cockpit to see how we operated the beast. And lengthy layovers were not unusual which always gave me an opportunity to see parts of the world which I had never visited before. On this trip, we subsequently flew back to London, with the same stops as those on the outward journey, arriving back in London on May 11 after an idyllic five days in Pakistan.

The VC 10 had three Flight Crew (Captain, Co-Pilot and Flight Engineer) and five Stewards and/or Stewardesses, as the Cabin Crew were then called. Fortunately for me, there was another crew member who also wished to do some exploring and so, once we arrived in Rawalpindi, we decided to head to the Khyber Pass and also to a village known as Dara Adamkhel before visiting the Valley of Swat.

The Khyber Pass, at 3,510 feet, has always been a gateway for various invasions and was part of the Silk Road between what is now Pakistan and Afghanistan. The First Anglo-Afghan War of 1839 saw action through the Pass and it became an important conduit in 2001 when the US invaded Afghanistan and 75% of NATO supplies were moved from Karachi to Peshawar, both in Pakistan, and on through the Pass to Kabul in Afghanistan.

Grabbing a taxi, I and the other crew member headed towards the important town in the Khyber Pass named Landi Kotal which was 150 miles from Rawalpindi where we were staying for our five day stopover. Driving in that part of Pakistan is nothing if not interesting as there appears to be no Rules of the Road with cars driving on the left, on the right and in the middle of the narrow, tortuous, mountain roads - and often numerous cows! But we made it to Landi Kotal in one piece and headed straight to the bazaar (the marketplace). There, the products of choice were every form of firearm imaginable from rifles to tiny pistols. A very popular pistol was one in the form of a fountain pen where the bullet was fired by pressing the clip on the side of the pen. Needless to say, we were talked into firing one of these "pens" which we duly did by holding it at arm's length with the bullet being fired vertically into the air with no comments being made by adjacent shoppers as this was a common sales practice. We also rode to the Pass itself where we could see into Afghanistan and the city of Jalalabad.

After Landi Kotal, we asked our friendly taxi driver to take us to the village of Dara Adamkhel which is where all types of firearms are manufactured and then sold in nearby villages, such as Landi Kotal. It was fascinating to see the many individuals sitting cross legged on the ground making these weapons from metal scraps with the end results looking exactly like the products manufactured by Western and Russian companies.

After returning to Rawalpindi and spending a delightful day in this attractive city, we decided to head to the Valley of Swat which involved another taxi ride of 150 miles. Swat is known as the Switzerland of Pakistan with the town sitting in the Valley at a height of around 3,200 feet surrounded by the gorgeous mountain range known as the Hindu Kush where the highest peak is approximately 19,500 feet. We spent time in the town and drove to a height of around 13,000 feet which was the highest non-aviating altitude I had been to to date. This was subsequently surpassed when I hiked to the top of what had once been the highest ski area in the world - Chacaltaya - at around 18,000 feet in Bolivia. Other memories of Swat were the delightful food in the bazaars, the friendly villagers and the local kids all hitting circular rotating hoops with sticks in what is known as "hoop rolling", or "trundling", as they ran around the village in groups seeing who could keep their hoop the longest from falling over.

Then the fun was over and we flew back to Blighty the way we had come, with another night in Amman, after an idyllic five days in Pakistan. Airline flying for Flight and Cabin Crews is sadly not the same these days - nor is it for passengers - and I'm very grateful that I flew in those far more hospitable days in a delightful aircraft with time to explore so many countries and to enjoy being with delightful passengers.

Sharq

Many years ago, my wife, Lisa, and I partnered with another couple in England and registered an import company specialising in ladies clothing made from natural fibres. We gave our company the name of **Chasric** since my partner was **Char**le**s** and I was **Ric**hard. The plan was to "sell" our imported products to our ladies boutique which we were planning to open in the small town of Wokingham in Berkshire to the west of London. As the majority of our imports would initially be shipped from India and the East, we decided to call the name of our boutique Sharq which is an Arabic word meaning East or Sun.

Charlie and I had met on a flying course with British Overseas Airways Corporation (BOAC) in London when we had both decided to try our hand at airline flying after our time as military fighter pilots. Charlie had flown the English Electric Lightning with the Royal Air Force and I had flown the F4 Phantom with the Royal Navy and United States Navy.

Charlie had been born in British Guiana to English parents but his family had moved to Wilton Connecticut where he went to high school before heading to the University of Denver. Unfortunately, he didn't last long at Denver due to a thirst for gambling and so, when his family moved to England, he decided to become a pilot with the Royal Air Force after marrying his

Australian wife, Lyn, who had been born in Melbourne in the state of Victoria. At the time that we started Chasric and Sharq, Lisa and I were living in the town of Fleet in Hampshire, not far from Wokingham, and Charlie and Lyn lived close by - with Charlie and I flying as pilots around the world with British Airways (BA), as BOAC had now become.

Charlie and I had earlier used our flights when flying with BOAC to make a little extra cash on the side by selling golf club grips to Indian golf clubs, where grips were in short supply, and, with the money earned, buying Indian made cricket bats in Bombay and Calcutta and selling them in England where they were more expensive. Forming Chasric seemed a natural progression and our wives were thrilled to have access to beautiful garments made from wool and silk.

Charlie's family had a contact in India who had fallen on hard times and was looking to increase his income by forming an export clothing company specialising in ladies clothing made from natural fibres. Iqbal Khan, Nawab of Palanpur, had had his land confiscated by the Indian Government and was living in Bombay - now called Mumbai. Palanpur is in the State of Gujarat in northeastern India and the title of Nawab would have been translated as Viceroy in British Colonial days.

Lisa and I flew to Bombay to meet up with Iqbal, as Charlie and Lyn also did, in order to inspect Iqbal's samples and to place an order for his clothing. The samples he showed us were of a high quality but, sadly, the clothing that subsequently arrived in England, after we'd placed our orders, left a lot to be desired and we soon had to find another source of natural fibres.

However, being with Iqbal and his wife was an extraordinary experience since he was still attempting to live the life of the Raj - albeit in a shabby apartment in the depths of Bombay.

He still had a chauffeur, although his car was a ratty old Morris Ambassador, and Iqbal always dressed as if he was off to Royal Ascot or perhaps to a garden party at Buckingham Palace. White trousers - not unlike cricket flannels - navy blue blazer, colourful cravat, flowing silk handkerchief in the outside pocket of his navy blue blazer and brogue shoes. While in Bombay, when Lisa and I were staying at the Taj Mahal Hotel, a friendly Indian we had met in the hotel, invited us to attend a sumptuous wedding being held on the grounds of this exquisite hotel. Our dress apparel for the wedding paled into insignificance compared to the beautiful and colourful clothing worn by the other guests and the highlight was when the bridegroom arrived riding a beautiful white horse.

Once we discovered that Iqbal's products were not up to snuff, we found another source of Indian clothing which was very popular in England at the time. So Charlie and Lisa, our official buyers, headed to the town of Slough near Heathrow Airport and visited an Indian wholesale import business selling exactly what we were looking for and this supplier became the new source of our products. At the same time, we had also decided to expand our tentacles and we started buying attractive clothing from Peru made of wool from alpaca and vicuna which are cousins of the llama. We also imported beautiful batik clothing from Indonesia.

Now that we'd arranged sources for our clothing, it was time to open our first shop - Sharq - in Wokingham. Luckily, we stumbled on a vacant space in a good location on a busy street, wooed a friendly bank manager to give us a loan and away we went. We hired a young girl to be our store manager while Charlie and Lisa continued to purchase the clothing and I found myself as the bookkeeper, working with a friendly accountant who was able to make sure that we paid no taxes. We did not pay ourselves any salaries but purchased an ancient bright red tiny Austin Mini as our company car which we ran at company expense and our two ladies had free access to all the delightful clothing. The Mini did its job although it had a large hole in the floorboard between the driver and the front seat passenger which allowed water from the streets to sometimes soak the driver's and passenger's feet.

Our business went quite well so we decided to open a second Sharq in the town of Henley-on-Thames, home of the Henley Royal Regatta, and we hired another young lady to act as manager. Sadly, her performance was not up to snuff and we had to politely ask her to stand down.

We also delighted in having fashion shows at various locations where Charlie would be the Master of Ceremonies, our wives and another lady friend, a New Zealander, would act as models and I would be the general gofer making sure that all was in order before these fun events. It was also very important that the four of us hold regular Board Meetings which we did at one of our two houses but not because we needed to have serious discussions about our business. Instead, these meetings became an excuse to have a sumptuous Indian dinner washed down with the occasional glass of wine and the odd gin and tonic.

After four years of fun and games, BA decided to give fully paid furlough to a number of pilots, including Charlie and me, and we decided to close up our shops and move on to something different. After paying off our bank loan, I got a job as a pilot with St Lucia Airways, while still being paid by BA, so Lisa and I, and our then two kids, headed to the Caribbean before moving to the USA when BA offered me early retirement.

Meanwhile, Charlie and Lyn moved to Melbourne where Charlie found himself a job with a local radio station before becoming a star news and sportscaster on national television. He was so popular and successful that he was asked to cover the Los Angeles Olympics in 1984 with the retired Australian tennis ace, John Newcome. Charlie was a first class golfer and squash player but he sadly died of a sudden heart attack in 2018 leaving Lisa and me with very happy memories of our days as amateur shop owners and of Charlie's wonderful humour and gift of the gab. We always knew he'd make a brilliant showman having listened to his amazing presentations at our fashion shows where his subtle sense of humour and his manner of speech always resulted in far more sales than our products justified!

Bangladesh

Bangladesh, the eighth most populated country in the world with over 167 million people, is surrounded by India to the west, north and east and by Myanmar, along a corridor on the Bay of Bengal, to the southeast. Its population is approximately 90% Muslim and 9% Hindu and the name Bangladesh means "Land of Bengal".

Originally named East Pakistan after the Indian subcontinent's independence from British rule in 1947, it broke away from what was then West Pakistan after a brutal civil war in 1971 when India gave military support to the formation of the independent country now known as Bangladesh.

Bangladesh, where the majority of the landscape is at a very low level and the highest point of land is only around 3,000 feet, has over 700 rivers and is under constant threat of flooding. There are approximately 5,000 miles of navigable waterways which are dominated by four large rivers - the Ganges, the Brahmaputra, the Meghna and the Padma - which all flow southwards into the Ganges Delta and out into the Bay of Bengal and on into the Indian Ocean through what are known as the Sundarbans - a complex of swamps, marshes, tidal streams, mudflats and small islands of mangrove forests with tigers, crocodiles and pythons. The production of 70% of the world's jute is the main source of income for many Bangladeshis and the capital city is Dhaka - originally spelled Dacca.

The stability of Bangladesh has been under pressure for some years due to the influx of Rohingya refugees from Myanmar (Burma) who have faced genocide for many years. Approximately 9,000 Rohingya refugees are now living in crowded camps in eastern Bangladesh.

Many years ago, there was a Bangladeshi restaurant in the town of Fleet in Hampshire in England - Fleet being the town I was born in and where my wife, Lisa, and I and our two daughters lived for approximately ten years in the 1970s. This restaurant sat close to The Oatsheaf pub, which features in Chapter Two of my book entitled "Flying through Life - From Fighter Pilot to Peace Activist", and was named Gulshan. Gulshan means "Rose Garden" and the delightful young owner was named Nur Moni which I believe translates into "Silent Light".

This was the time that I was a pilot with British Overseas Airways Corporation (BOAC) flying international routes all over the world except to West Africa and South America. Dhaka was often one of my destinations - flying there via Beirut, Tehran, Karachi, New Delhi, Bombay (Mumbai) or Calcutta (Kolkata).

Nur Moni had a sister in Dhaka who was married to a gentleman named Bulbul who owned a Honda dealership. I learned that Bulbul meant Nightingale which was rather ironic since the nightingale sings a beautiful song at night especially during the breeding season. Ironic because Bulbul was always asking me to introduce him to the prettiest stewardess (flight attendant) in our crew when I visited with him and his wife during my often lengthy stopovers in Bangladesh! The reason I got to know Bulbul and his wife was because Nur Moni would always ask me to take various items with me as gifts for his sister. This was in pre-9/11 days when the flight deck door was always open and I was able to transport items across the world with me on the flight deck and not have to check such baggage into the hold.

Apart from being entertained by Bulbul, there was always time for exploration on the many waterways since our crew stopovers were often up to three nights - something that does not occur in today's airline world. Due to the preponderance of waterways, ancient ferries, some known as "Rockets", plied up and down the rivers as the main means of public transportation. The name of "Rocket" for some of these ferries was a bit of a joke since, although they were faster than the other means of waterborne conveyance, they were hardly speedy.

On one trip, I and three other crew members decided to try out this means of waterborne propulsion so we took a long round trip ferry ride to the town of Barisal about 75 miles to the south of Dhaka. Our ferry, named "Ostrich", had been built in 1929 on Clydebank in Scotland and riding on it and visiting Barisal was like going back in time. Having gone through endless post-British colonial bureaucracy in buying the very cheap tickets which cost the equivalent of $2 for the round trip, we boarded this delightful old ferry and enjoyed the trip of a lifetime. Service onboard was extremely polite and efficient and the food we were served at no extra cost was first class and we were even given cabins so we could have a post prandial nap on the way back to Dhaka.

Apart from jute, bricks were an important source of income - as I believe they still are - and large numbers of bricks were shipped down river to Dhaka from the upstream kilns in flat bottomed wooden cargo boats powered only by square sails. These boats could only sail downwind and downstream with the current so getting the empty boats back up to the kilns was a different matter. With no engine, there was only one way to solve the problem. Tie a very long hawser to the top of the mast and employ up to 100 strong men who would tow the boat back home while plodding along the riverbank.

I always delighted in telling my Bangladeshi stories to Nur Moni on returning home while eating one of his delicious meals. Sadly, airline flying is no longer fun for both crew and passengers and I was fortunate to have experienced international travel in the days when family and friends could always ride with me on the flight deck. I wonder if those flat bottomed cargo boats are still being towed by hand up the tributaries of the Ganges and the Brahmaputra?

September 11, 2001

Early in the morning on September 11 2001, I drove from my home in Princeton Junction, New Jersey, to Port Liberte in Jersey City on the Hudson River and caught the ferry to the South Street Seaport on the East River in Lower Manhattan. This was my usual commute to my job as an Aviation Reinsurance Broker for a Lloyd's of London broking company and I arrived at my office in Wall Street Plaza around 8 am. My office was not far from the South Street Seaport.

Our office building was on Water Street, situated a short distance to the east of the World Trade Center (WTC), and I was due to have lunch that day at noon with an Aviation Reinsurance Underwriter in a restaurant in 1 WTC. If the events of that day - now known as 9/11 - had occurred approximately three hours later, I may not now be writing this story.

My own office faced west but I did not have a direct view of the WTC although other offices in my company, close to mine on the same floor, did. Around 8.45 am on that fateful day, I heard a loud bang which sounded to me like a large truck hitting a pothole on Water Street below my window. Almost immediately, my secretary came rushing into my office in a state of shock screaming that an aircraft had hit the WTC. Rushing to her office, I saw the second aircraft hit the tower and, like many others, my immediate reaction was that a small aircraft had hit this vast building. The enormous size of the WTC disguised the fact that the two aircraft, which had carried out these evil acts of death and destruction, were in fact large airliners.

Our eldest daughter, Shannon, who worked in midtown, immediately called me and suggested that I start walking north to her apartment on the Upper East Side. Meanwhile, she had called my wife, Lisa, in Princeton Junction to say that I was OK and that I would be spending the night in New York City with her. Shortly thereafter, all means of telephonic communication disappeared and my company decided to abandon our building. I was therefore no longer able to speak to Lisa or Shannon.

Having initially gathered on Water Street in front of our building, it was then decided it was safe to go back up to our floor in Wall Street Plaza to gather our belongings although we could see the tremendous destruction and fires not far away. But on going back to our floor, the first tower of the WTC collapsed and a wave of white powder came flowing eastwards down Maiden Lane towards us due to the westerly wind. This mass of white powder covered our building and it was decided to escape our offices and for everyone to find their own way back home as best they could. Some of my fellow workmates decided to start walking northwards and it took a number of them up to three days to get back to their homes in Connecticut since no public transportation, including the subway, was available.

However, I decided to go over to the South Street Seaport and take whatever ferry was running - regardless of where it would be heading. By this time, I was unable to call Shannon and Lisa to tell them that I would not now be heading north in Manhattan but would be attempting to get home. Amazingly, the Seaport was now a fleet of ferries carrying out a Dunkirk style evacuation for all of us trying to escape the distressing situation and my luck was in as the ferry I boarded was in fact going to Port Liberte where my car was parked from my morning commute. As my ferry rounded the lower end of Manhattan, we all, shockingly, had a grandstand view of the second tower collapsing but I, and the other passengers, made it back safely to where our cars were parked in Jersey City and I started the drive back home.

But first I had to attempt to notify Shannon that I would not be coming to her apartment and also let Lisa know that I was in fact heading home in one piece. Surprisingly, I was able to call our son, Rich, at university in Colorado and tell him the story and he was able, after a number of attempts, to call New York and New Jersey and notify his sister and his mother that I was now heading home. Lisa got the message about five minutes before I walked in the door.

Driving home, I suspect I was in a state of shock and I was not aware that the suit I was wearing that day was covered in all that white powder. I was also desperately thirsty and, exiting the New Jersey Turnpike close to Cranbury, New Jersey, I decided to go to Teddy's Diner to get some water. Walking into Teddy's, I was greeted by Teddy himself who looked as if he'd seen a ghost! I was the first person to arrive in Cranbury who had been at the scene of the disaster and he gave me, not just water, but a delicious breakfast as well - all on the house. So I made it safely back home in one piece with Lisa fortunately having learned about my arrival a few minutes before I showed up. Not long after I arrived home, the telephone rang and it was a young Frenchman, Didier, who was on a train in Italy, calling to see if I was OK. It was the first call I got that day and Didier had earlier lived with us for a period as a teenager in order to learn English.

I was indeed one of the fortunate ones who survived the ordeal, unlike a number of business acquaintances who worked in the WTC and also Todd Beamer, from Cranbury, who was so sadly killed with all the other passengers when his hijacked airliner crashed in Pennsylvania. All of us at my company, who had been there on the day, were subsequently medically examined to make sure that we had not been infected by the white powder and we were all counselled to make sure that we had not been mentally affected, or had PTSD, by what we had gone through. Of course, my experience on 9/11 paled into insignificance compared to those who were in the WTC and didn't live to fight another day and those who managed to escape the flaming building itself.

SPLASH

SPLASH is the acronym for **S**tudent **P**articipation in **L**earning **A**quatic **S**cience and **H**istory and it was the brainchild of the former Princeton University Professor Bart Hoebel (1935-2011). She was a 58 foot long steam powered stern paddlewheeler and a replica of similar vessels built in the 1880s.

SPLASH weighed 15 tons, was 50 feet in length with an 8 feet wide paddle at the stern, had three passenger decks which could accommodate 35 passengers and crew and was inspected on an annual basis by the US Coast Guard. The fuel used to generate the steam to power the vessel was diesel (No 2 Home Heating Fuel) contained in a 90 gallon fuel tank. The steam operated at 125 psi at a temperature of 350 degrees fahrenheit.

The two engines, which were double acting, reciprocating and non-condensing, each operated at five horsepower and the operating cycle was by pump from fuel tank to boiler to steam to the engines with the water being drawn from the Delaware River and the resulting precipitation from the condensed steam, at the end of the cycle, returning into the river.

Flat bottomed keel boats were used on major rivers, with no power, before steamboats came into being and these powerless boats were either hauled by hand back up river at the end of the trip or broken up or sold -

with the crew having to walk back upstream. These trips would take up to nine months.

In 1769, the Scotsman, James Watt, invented the steam engine and, in the USA, John Fitch built a steamboat in 1787 but it proved to be too expensive. However, the first successful steamboat was the "Claremont" built by Robert Fulton in Lancaster County, Pennsylvania, in 1807. Fulton's steamboat's first voyage was on the Hudson River from New York City to Albany, New York - a trip of 40 miles which took eight hours at a speed of six knots - or five mph. Fulton then moved to London and on to France where he met a steamboat inventor named Robert Livingston. Another Englishman, Thomas Newcomen, had developed an important invention - the atmospheric steam powered pump - in 1712.

Another individual in the development of the steam powered paddlewheeler was Elijah McCoy, born in 1844. His parents were fugitive slaves who escaped from Kentucky to Canada where Elijah was born and his early employment was in machine shops in the USA where he had moved for employment and he invented an automatic lubricator for oiling steam engines. A skilled craftsman, he was notable for 57 U.S. patents and his lubricating invention and his name became a popular expression - "The Real McCoy" - since steam operators only wanted the real thing and not some imitation.

SPLASH was docked at a jetty on the Delaware River a few hundred yards to the south of the Lambertville Station on the New Jersey side. The Delaware is the longest river to the east of the Mississippi River at 350 miles long and it supplies water for approximately 6% of the USA's population. The early Lenni Lenape Native Americans used canoes as ferries across the Delaware with boats being rowed across the river commencing in 1717. The first bridge across the Delaware was not built until 1814.

SPLASH sadly ceased operating a few years ago and was sold to an individual in Alaska who sent a large truck and trailer to Lambertville, loaded up dear old SPLASH and carted her away to distant pastures in the 49th State. In its operating days, SPLASH had a Coast Guard qualified

Captain and Engineer plus a usual crew of five which included my role as the historian onboard.

The majority of the SPLASH outings on the Delaware involved heading up stream, sometimes anchoring, and then returning to her dock at the end of a fun day. Education was at the forefront of each trip and the passengers were mainly school children with older club groups sometimes enjoying the river while onboard. SPLASH also took the public for rides on the river during the Shad Festival which is held annually in Lambertville.

The three decks allowed groups to be divided into three with one group on the foredeck, one on the lower deck next to the engines and one on the upper deck. Each group would spend time on each deck learning a specific topic before rotating in turn to the other decks and learning about other subjects.

Subjects taught were River Chemistry Testing, the History of the Delaware during the Revolutionary War, the Operation of the Steam Engine, Bird Watching and River Pollution. The Chemistry exercise involved testing for such as pH/Acidity, Salinity, Water Temperature and Oxygen Turbidity on the foredeck while George Washington's many crossing of the Delaware were discussed in the History talk on the lower deck.

Apart from his famous crossing of the Delaware before the two Battles of Trenton and the Battle of Princeton, there was also the time Washington crossed the river at Coryell's Ferry (now Lambertville) after he and his troops had left Valley Forge in June 1778 and marched via Hopewell, Kingston and Cranbury and on to the Battle of Monmouth. I've calculated that Washington actually crossed the Delaware 11 times during the course of his life.

The Engineer, on the lower deck, gave an excellent talk on how the Steam Engine worked and Bird Watching was conducted on the upper deck with bird books and binoculars. But the exercise which the school kids enjoyed the most was the River Pollution demonstration. In this, a relief model of a typical river the size of the Delaware with its associated river banks and developments was used to show how the river can easily be polluted. This relief model had factories, tennis courts, swimming pools, garages etc and kids in turn were given a different coloured fluid to demonstrate pollution by pouring each fluid in turn onto the model to illustrate such as oil, gasoline, chlorine, waste water etc which subsequently flowed into the river. The piece de resistance came at the end when the last kid poured a bucket of water over it all to demonstrate rainfall and show how this pollution could indeed end up in the river. Fortunately, the pollution situation has been greatly improved and the Delaware River is cleaner today than it has been in the past.

Once SPLASH had docked and been put to bed at the end of a fun day, the crew repaired to the Lambertville Station for a well earned libation and an enjoyable debrief of the day's events. These were happy days and it's a shame that this wonderful and enlightening steamboat, and all it taught, is no longer ploughing the lovely Delaware River.

www.ingramcontent.com/pod-product-compliance
Lightning Source LLC
Chambersburg PA
CBHW061404140726
47997CB00003B/1360